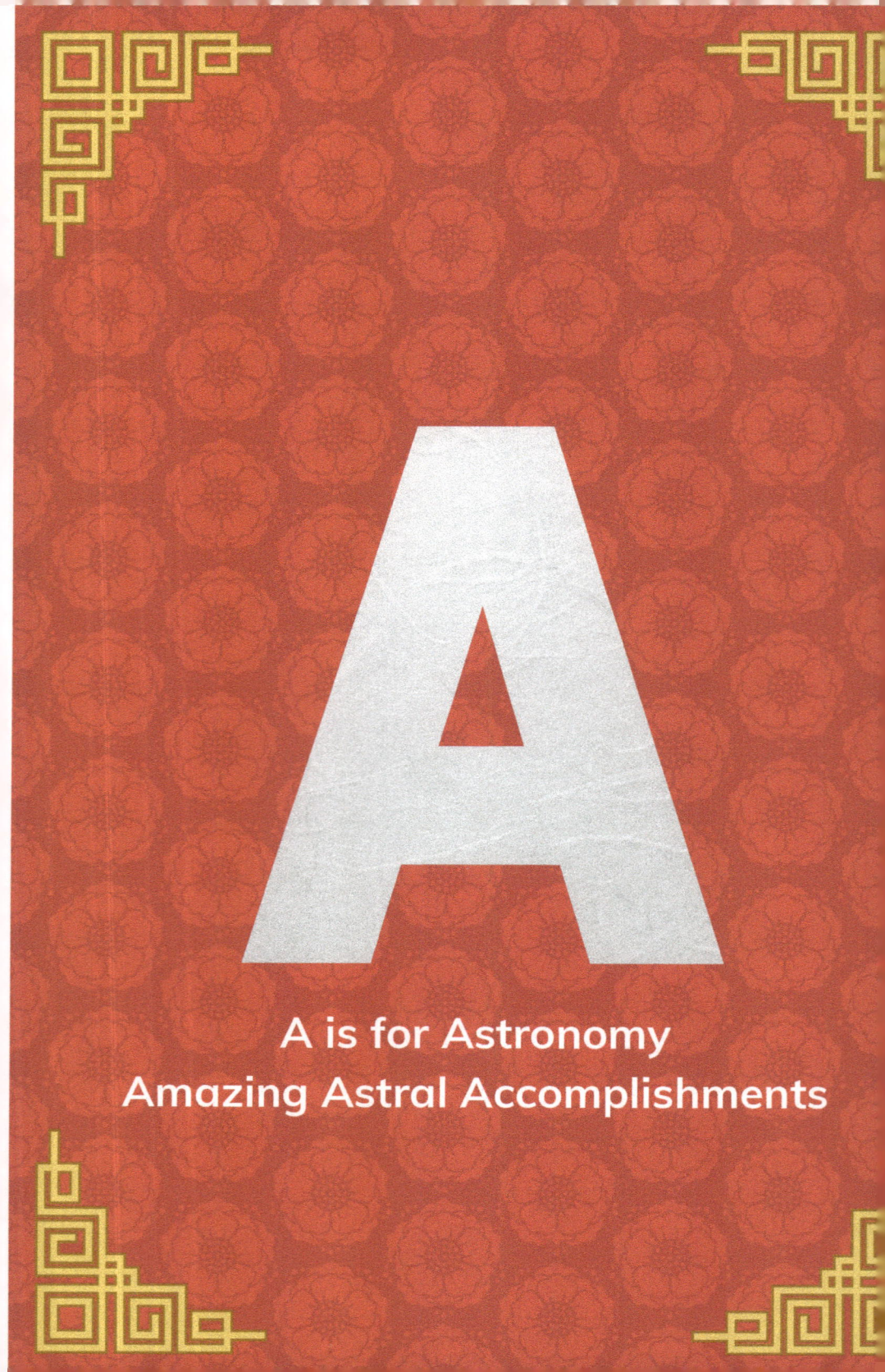

A

A is for Astronomy
Amazing Astral Accomplishments

Q is for Queen Seondeok

by History Unboxed®

Q is for Queen Seondeok: A Historic Alphabet Book
Text ©2025 History Unboxed
Cover ©2025 History Unboxed

Published by History Unboxed®
29 Culpeper Street
Warrenton VA 20186
www.historyunboxed.com

History Unboxed® and the History Unboxed logo are trademarks of History Unboxed.

Library of Congress Cataloging-in-Publication Data
Library of Congress Control Number: 2025933206

ISBN: 978-1-956571-25-7

For permissions, bulk paperback orders, or more information, please visit www.historyunboxed.com

Book Design by Stephanie Hanson
Lexile® Level: 690L

Image Credits
G is for Goguryeo
Korean ambassadors during a audience with king Varkhuman of Samarkand. 648-651 CE, Afrasiyab, Samarkand Photograph: Republic of Korea, CC BY-SA 2.0
H is for Hwangnhongsa
1:10 scale model of Hwangnyongsa. Gyeongju City, KOGL Type 1 via Wikimedia Commons
N is for Namsan
Thelesyl, CC BY-SA 4.0 <https://creativecommons.org/licenses/by-sa/4.0>, via Wikimedia Commons
R is for Royal
National Museum of Korea, KOGL Type 1
<http://www.kogl.or.kr/open/info/license_info/by.do>, via Wikimedia Commons
V is for Visionary
Adil, CC BY-SA 3.0 <https://creativecommons.org/licenses/by-sa/3.0>, via Wikimedia Commons

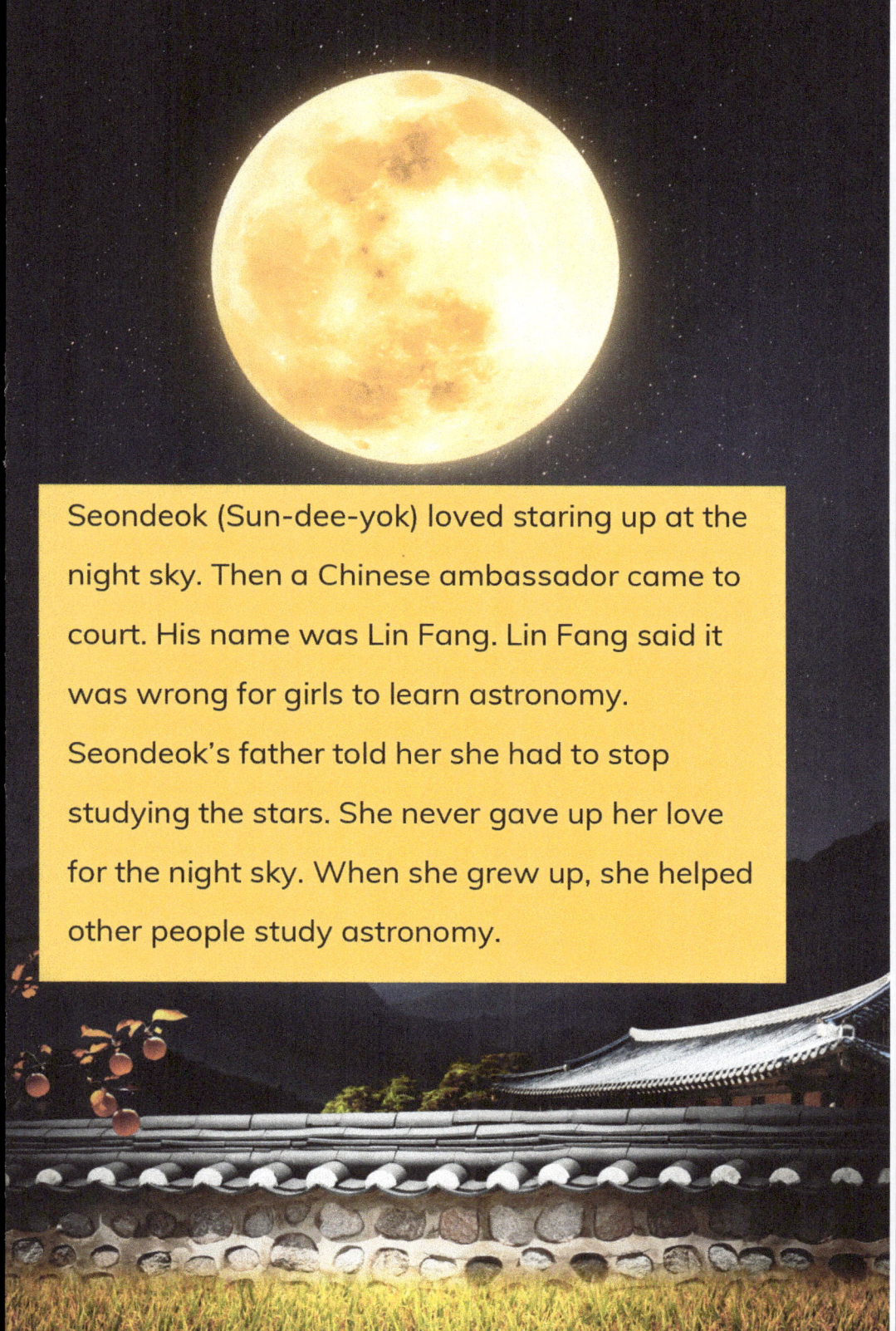

Seondeok (Sun-dee-yok) loved staring up at the night sky. Then a Chinese ambassador came to court. His name was Lin Fang. Lin Fang said it was wrong for girls to learn astronomy. Seondeok's father told her she had to stop studying the stars. She never gave up her love for the night sky. When she grew up, she helped other people study astronomy.

B

B is for Bone Rank
Born into Sacred Bone

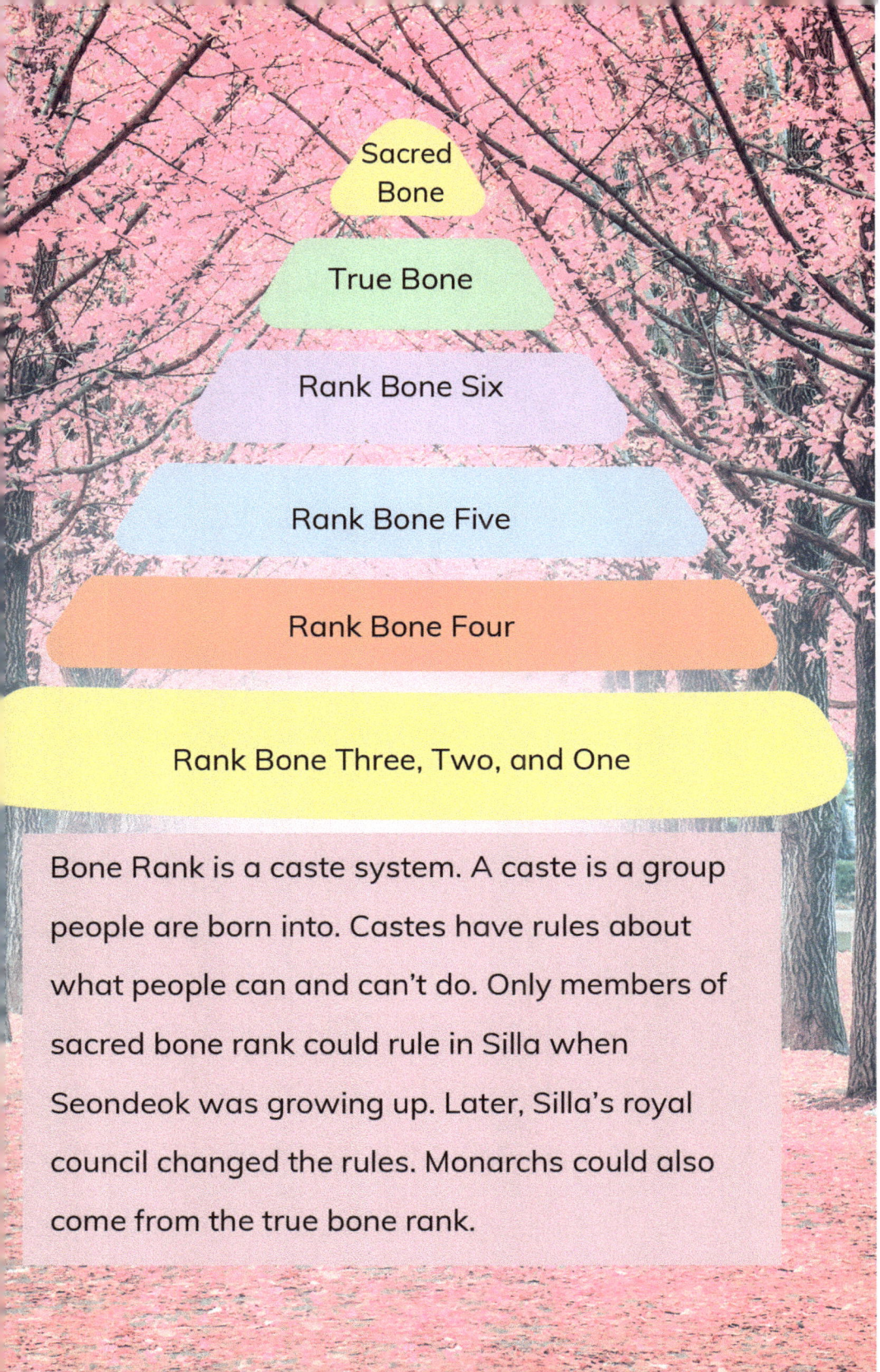

Sacred Bone

True Bone

Rank Bone Six

Rank Bone Five

Rank Bone Four

Rank Bone Three, Two, and One

Bone Rank is a caste system. A caste is a group people are born into. Castes have rules about what people can and can't do. Only members of sacred bone rank could rule in Silla when Seondeok was growing up. Later, Silla's royal council changed the rules. Monarchs could also come from the true bone rank.

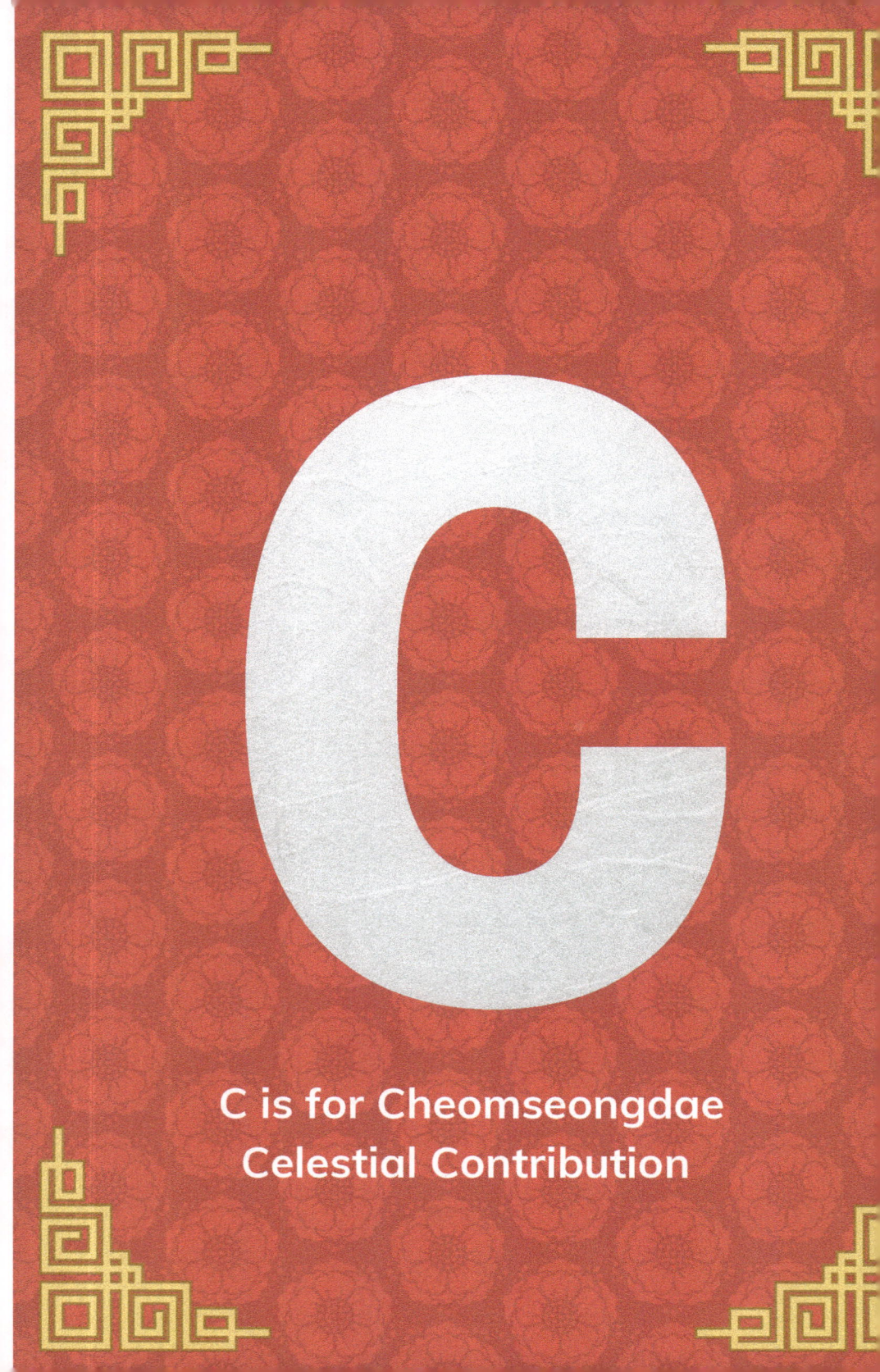

C

C is for Cheomseongdae
Celestial Contribution

Cheomseongdae (Chum-sung-day) is an observatory. It is a tower built for people to study the stars. The tower still stands today. Its name means "Reverently Regarding the Stars Platform." It is made of 365 granite blocks. There is one block for each day of the year. There are 27 rows because Seondeok was the 27th ruler of her kingdom.

D

D is for Deokman
Daughter of the King

Seondeok had many names. Her birth name was Deokman (Duck-mahn). When she was growing up, people called her Princess Deokman. She was a clever and caring girl.

E

E is for Empress
Enthroned and esteemed

Seondeok's people admired her. She said being a good leader meant helping others. When the kingdom needed rain, she helped her people work together. She sent help to hungry people in the country. Her people knew she cared about them.

F

F is for Female
First, fearless and formidable

Queen Seondeok was the first known queen in Asia. When her father died, there were no living males of sacred bone rank. The kingdom made her queen. She had to lead Silla against its rival kingdoms: Goguryeo (Go-goo-ry-oh) and Baekje (Beck-jay).

G

G is for Goguryeo
Glaringly greedy

Goguryeo was a rival kingdom. The king wanted to conquer Seondeok's kingdom, Silla. Seondeok sent her nephew to talk to King Bojang. The king locked her nephew up as a prisoner. Seondeok sent an army to rescue her nephew. King Bojang let his prisoner go instead of fighting the army.

Korean ambassadors during a audience with king Varkhuman of Samarkand. 648-651 CE.

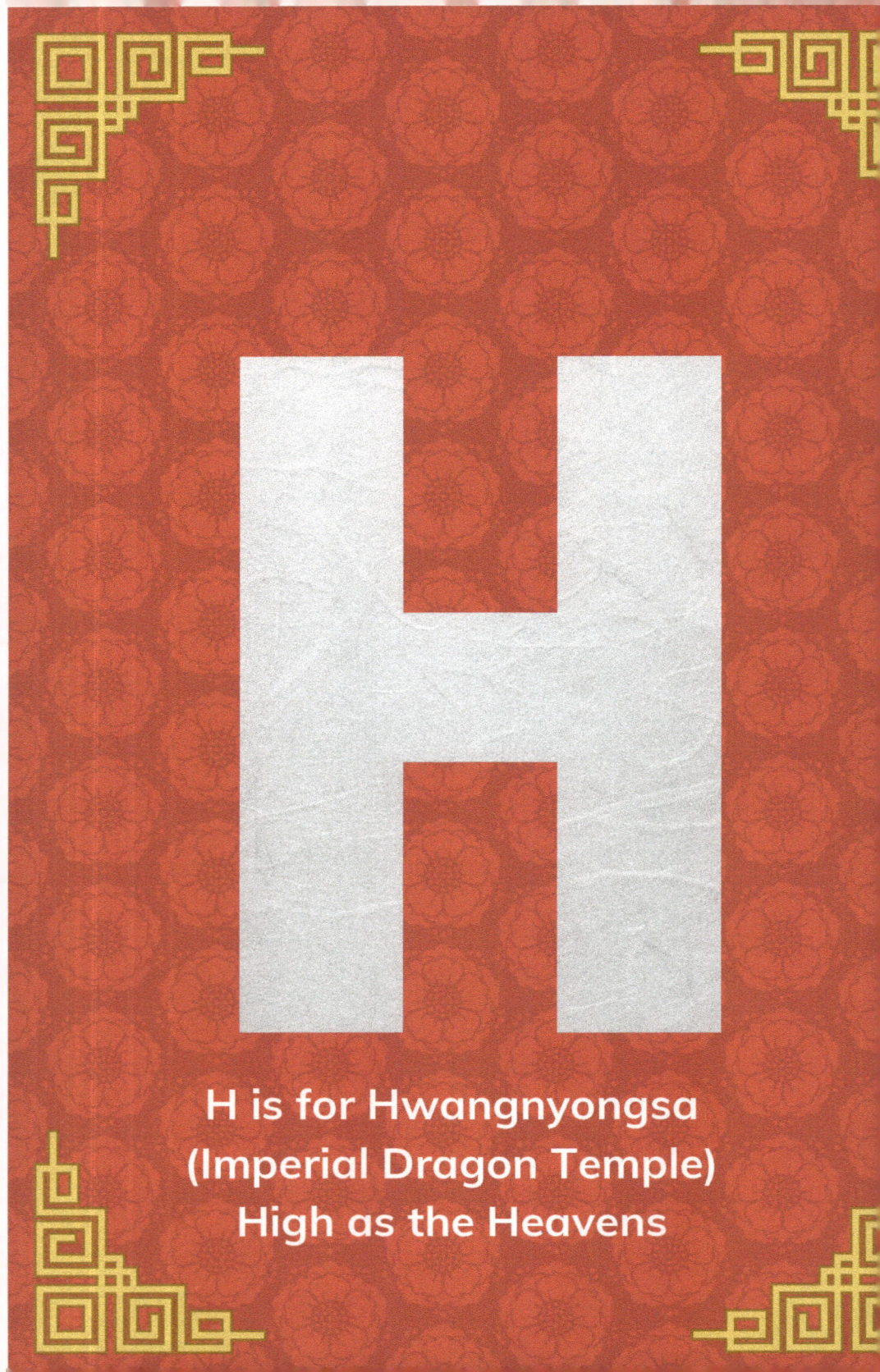

H

H is for Hwangnyongsa
(Imperial Dragon Temple)
High as the Heavens

Hwangnyongsa (whahng-neeyong-sah) was one of the tallest buildings in East Asia.

Its name means Imperial Dragon Temple. Legend says it stands on the spot where a yellow dragon appeared. The dragon promised Silla would destroy all its enemies.

I

**I is for Intelligent
Inspirational and Insightful**

Queen Seondeok loved learning. She knew knowledge made her kingdom stronger. In the 1100s, a Korean historian wrote she was "generous, benevolent, wise, and smart."

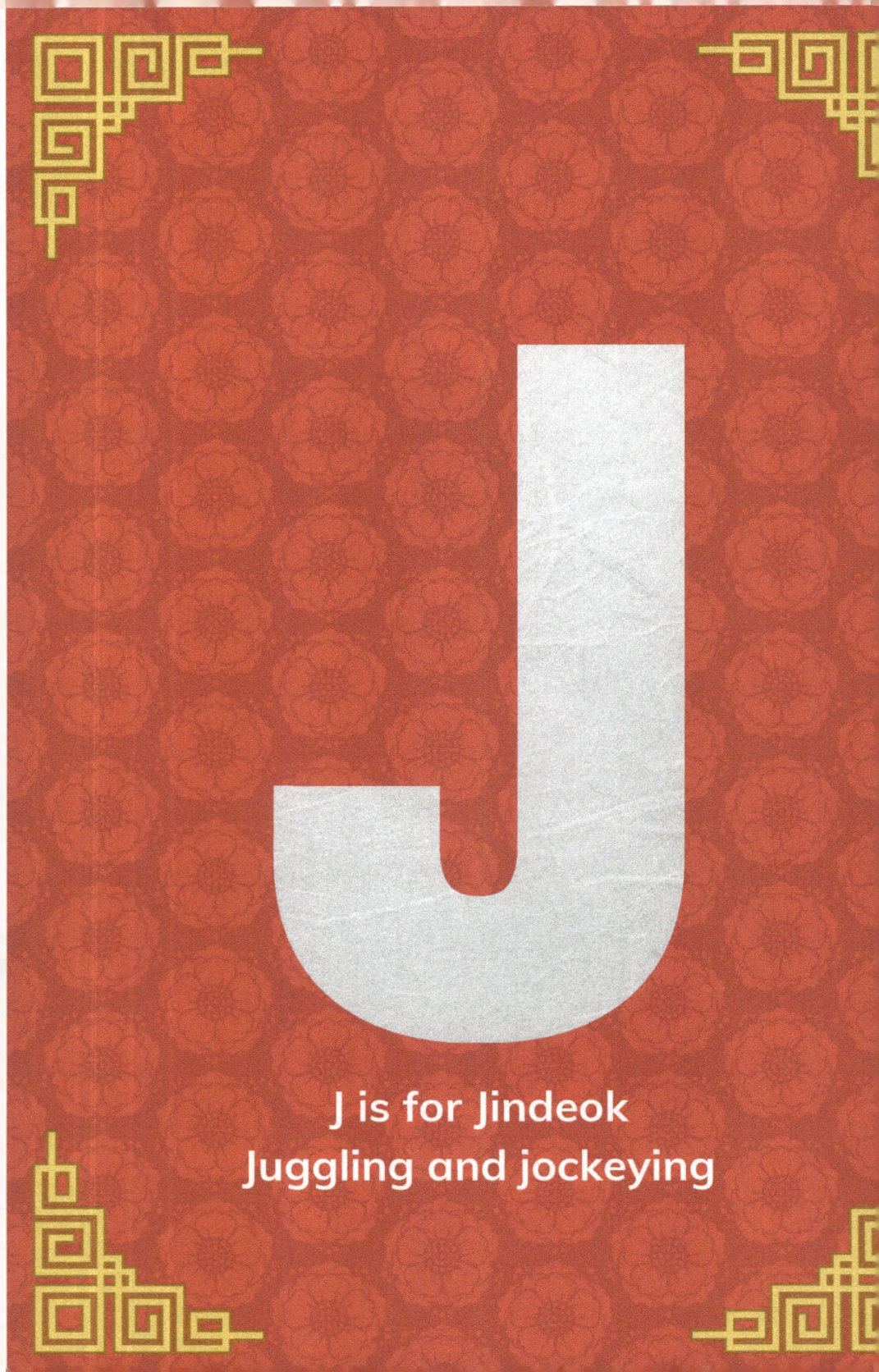

J

J is for Jindeok
Juggling and jockeying

Jindeok (Jin-duck) was Seondeok's female cousin. She ruled after Seondeok. Jindeok had to jockey for favor with the Tang court. She was the last ruler from the Sacred Bone Rank.

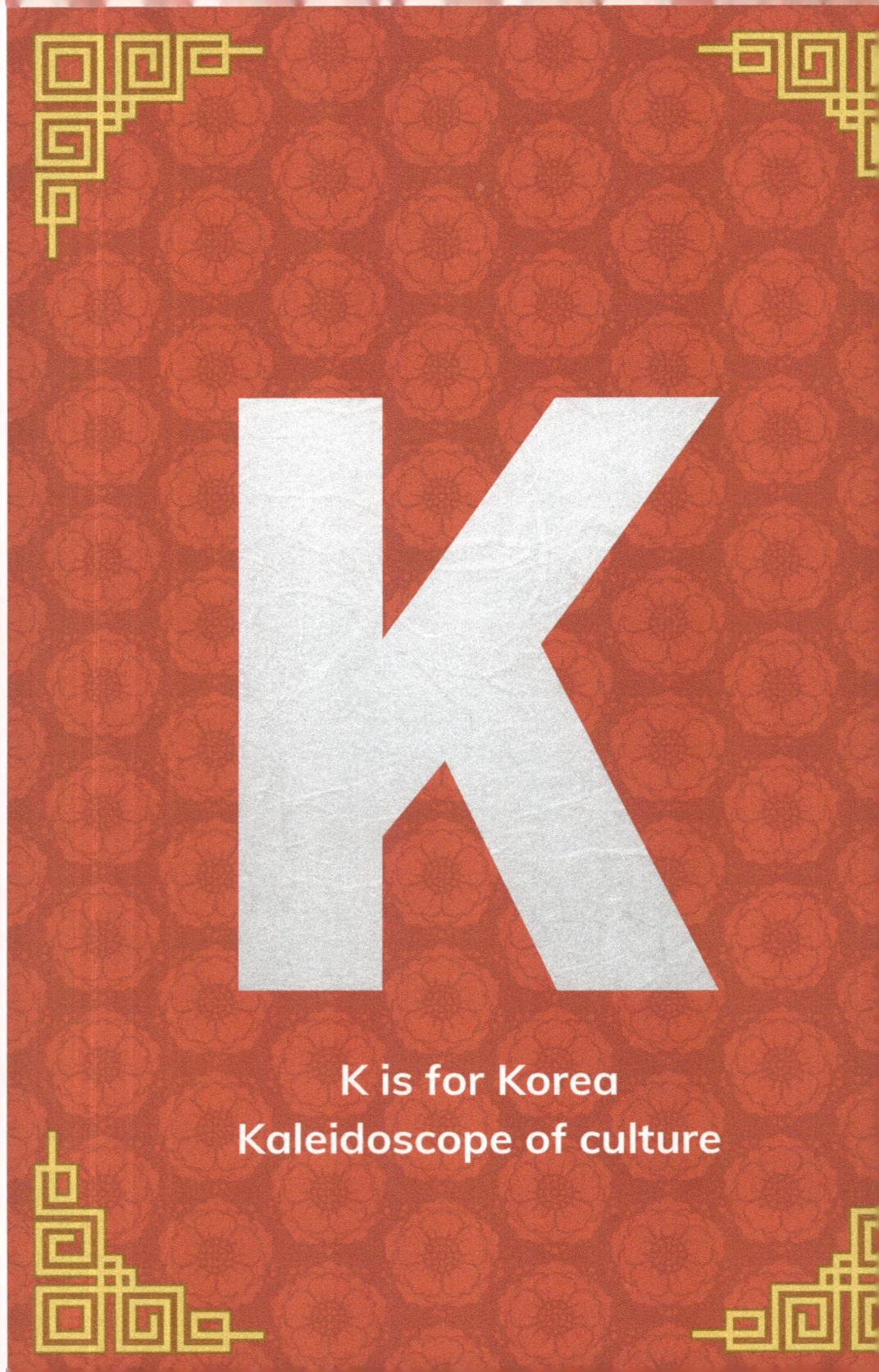

K

K is for Korea
Kaleidoscope of culture

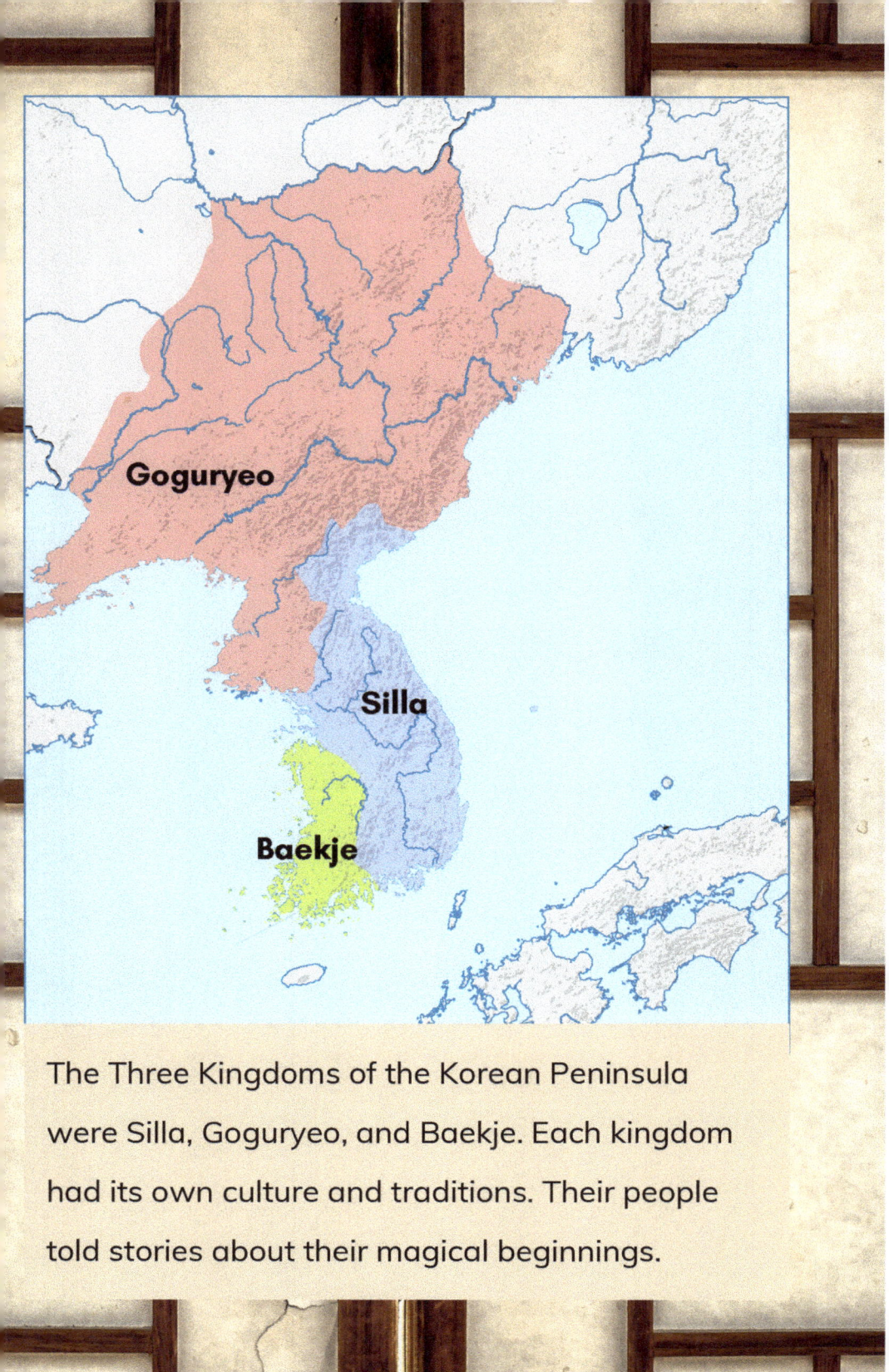

The Three Kingdoms of the Korean Peninsula were Silla, Goguryeo, and Baekje. Each kingdom had its own culture and traditions. Their people told stories about their magical beginnings.

L

L is for Legacy
Leadership and loyalty

Seondeok showed women could be strong, wise, and successful leaders. She inspired her people to be loyal. Her work as leader helped later rulers unite the Three Kingdoms after she died.

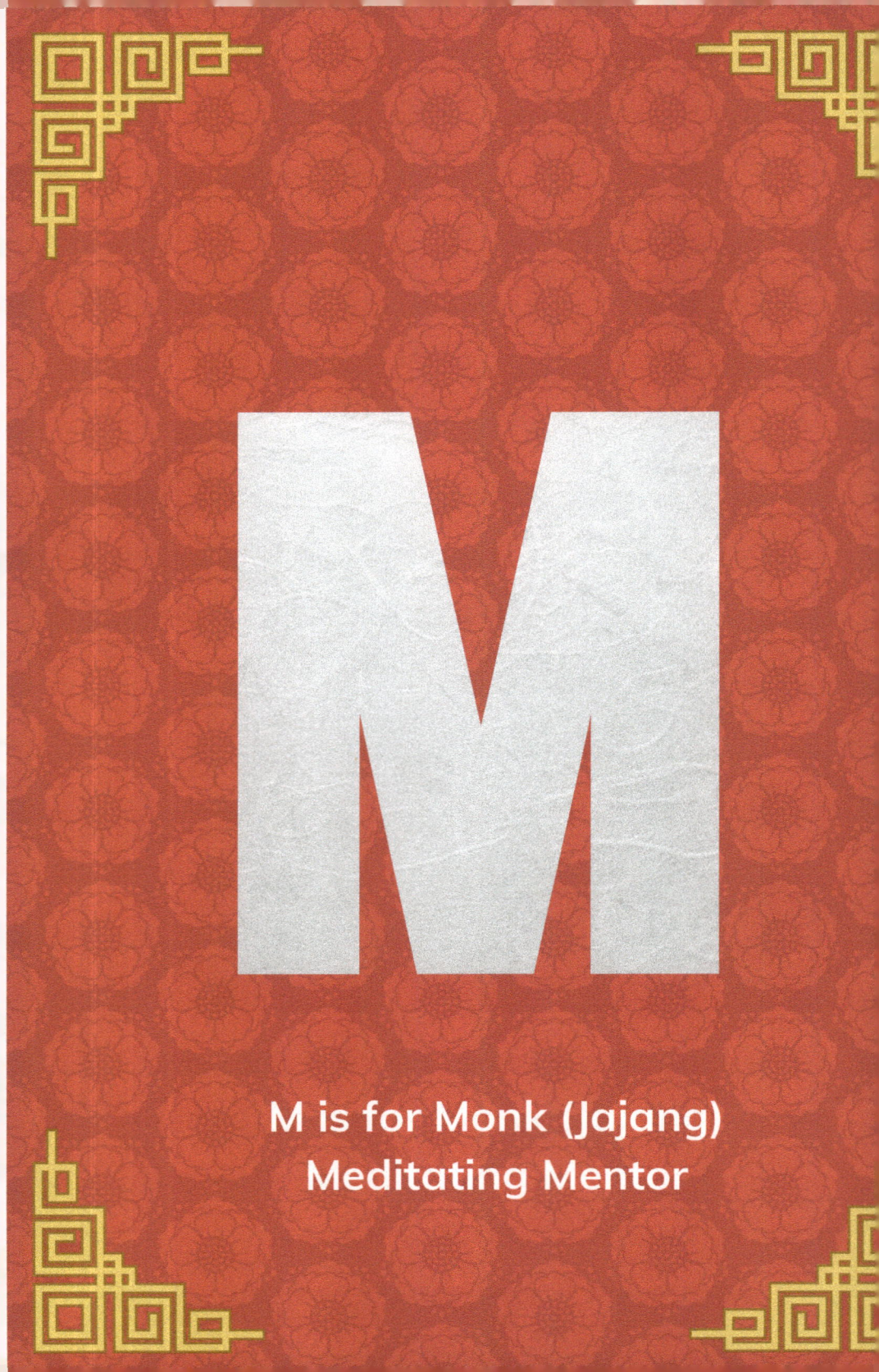

M

M is for Monk (Jajang)
Meditating Mentor

Jajang (Jah-jang) was a Buddhist monk who gave advice to Seondeok. Buddhism was important to Seondeok. Jajang told her to build a tall pagoda to calm her people.

Anonymous. Painting of Jajang. 1804.

N

N is for Namsan
Nestled in nature's nook

Namsan (Nahm-sawn) is a sacred mountain.

Many of Silla's rulers are buried there. Seondeok's

tomb is on the southern side of the mountain.

Tomb of Queen Seondeok

O

O is for Omens
Observed and obeyed

One night, Seondeok saw a new star in the sky. She said it meant something dangerous was coming. Seondeok told her advisors to be ready. Then her enemies started a rebellion.

P

P is for Peony
Parable of pink petals

Seondeok saw a Chinese painting of peonies. She said it was sad the pretty flowers did not have a scent. She could tell because there were no bees. The story showed her wisdom.

Painting by Chinese Dowager Empress Cixi

Q

Q is for Queen
Quelling quarrels with grace

Queen Seondeok tried to make peace instead of war. She tried to work out problems with other kingdoms before starting wars.

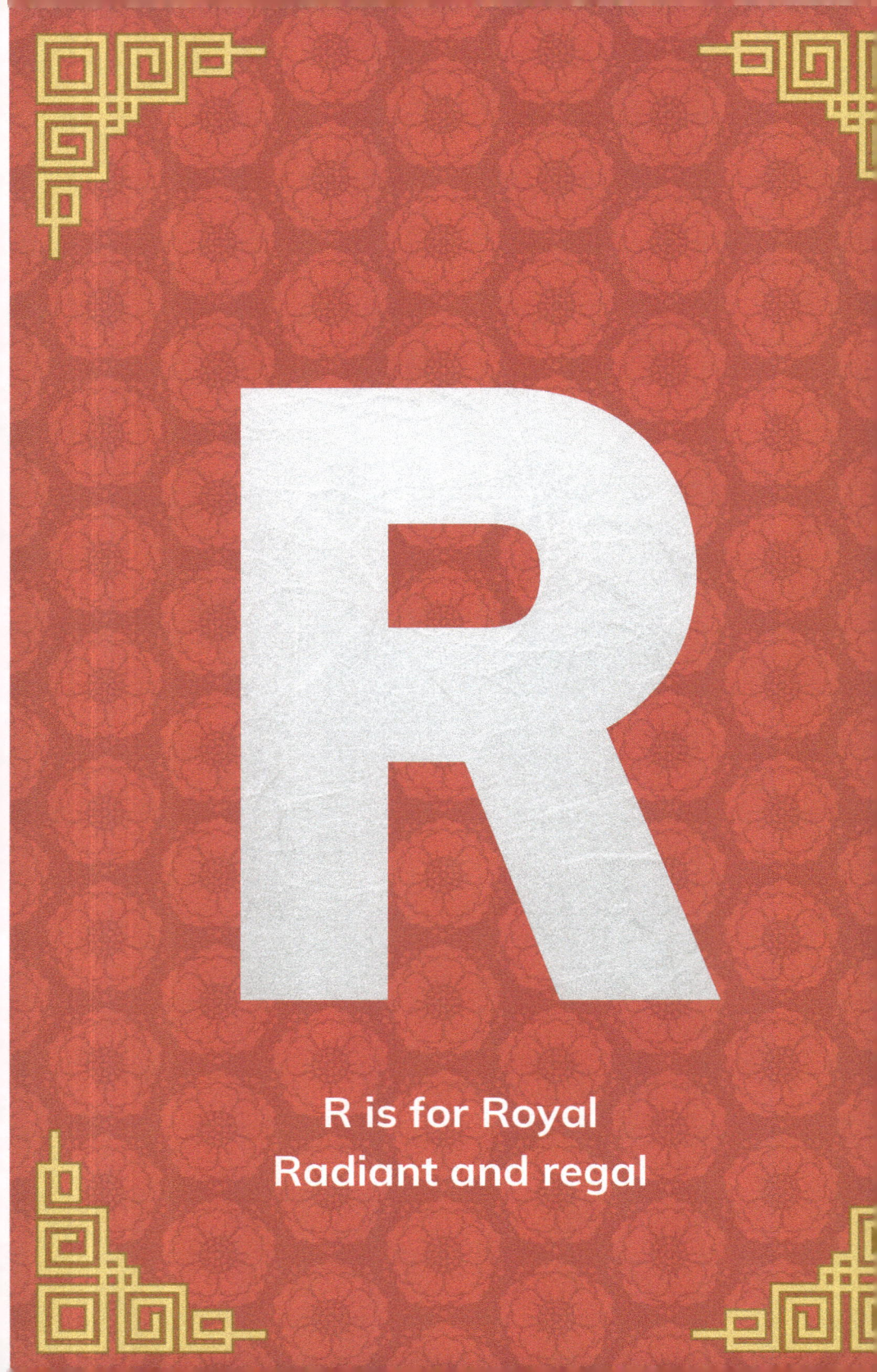

R

R is for Royal
Radiant and regal

Seondeok brought light to her kingdom. She showed kindness, intelligence, and dedication to her people. She was a graceful and noble queen.

S

S is for Silla
Sovereign and strong

Silla was one of the Three Kingdoms of Korea. A legend says the first ruler of Silla hatched from an egg laid by a white horse. The boy's name was Bak Hyeokgeose (Hyuk-gug-seh).

T

T is for Tang
Taunting Taizong

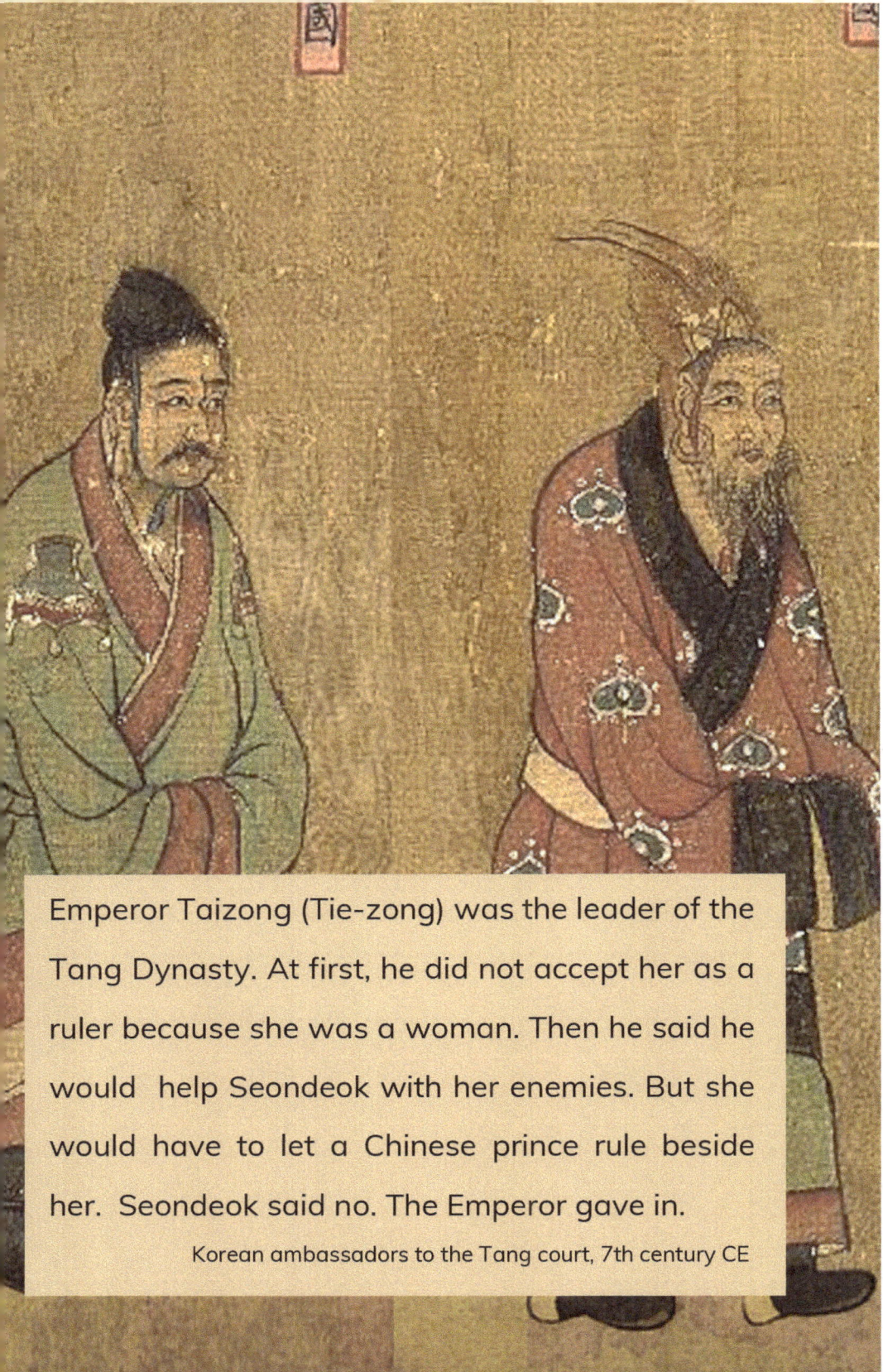

Emperor Taizong (Tie-zong) was the leader of the Tang Dynasty. At first, he did not accept her as a ruler because she was a woman. Then he said he would help Seondeok with her enemies. But she would have to let a Chinese prince rule beside her. Seondeok said no. The Emperor gave in.

Korean ambassadors to the Tang court, 7th century CE

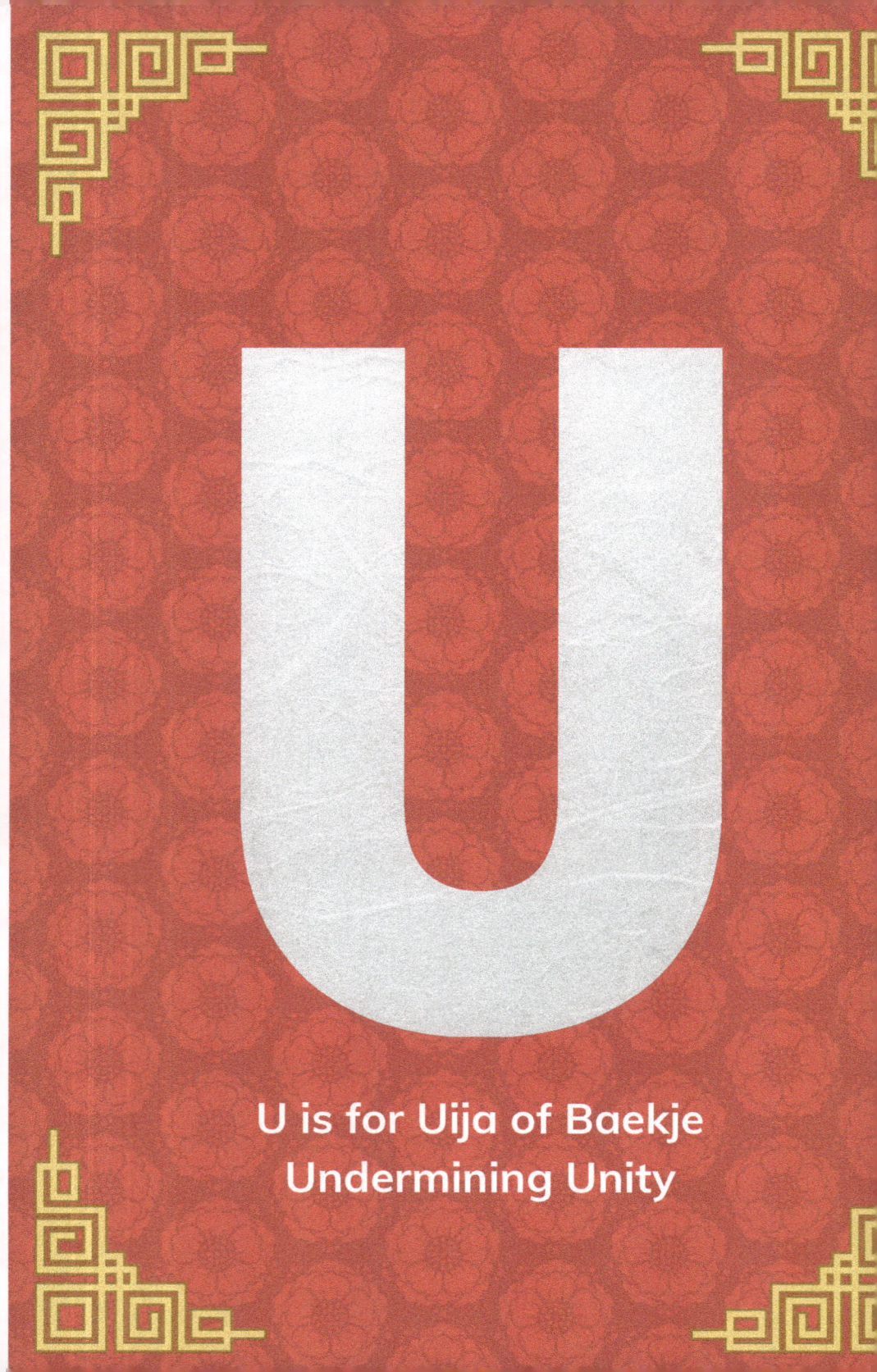

U

U is for Uija of Baekje
Undermining Unity

King Uija (Wee-jah) led the rival kingdom of Baekje against Seondeok. He lost his kingdom to Silla and the Chinese Tang Dynasty.

Baekje Cultural Center

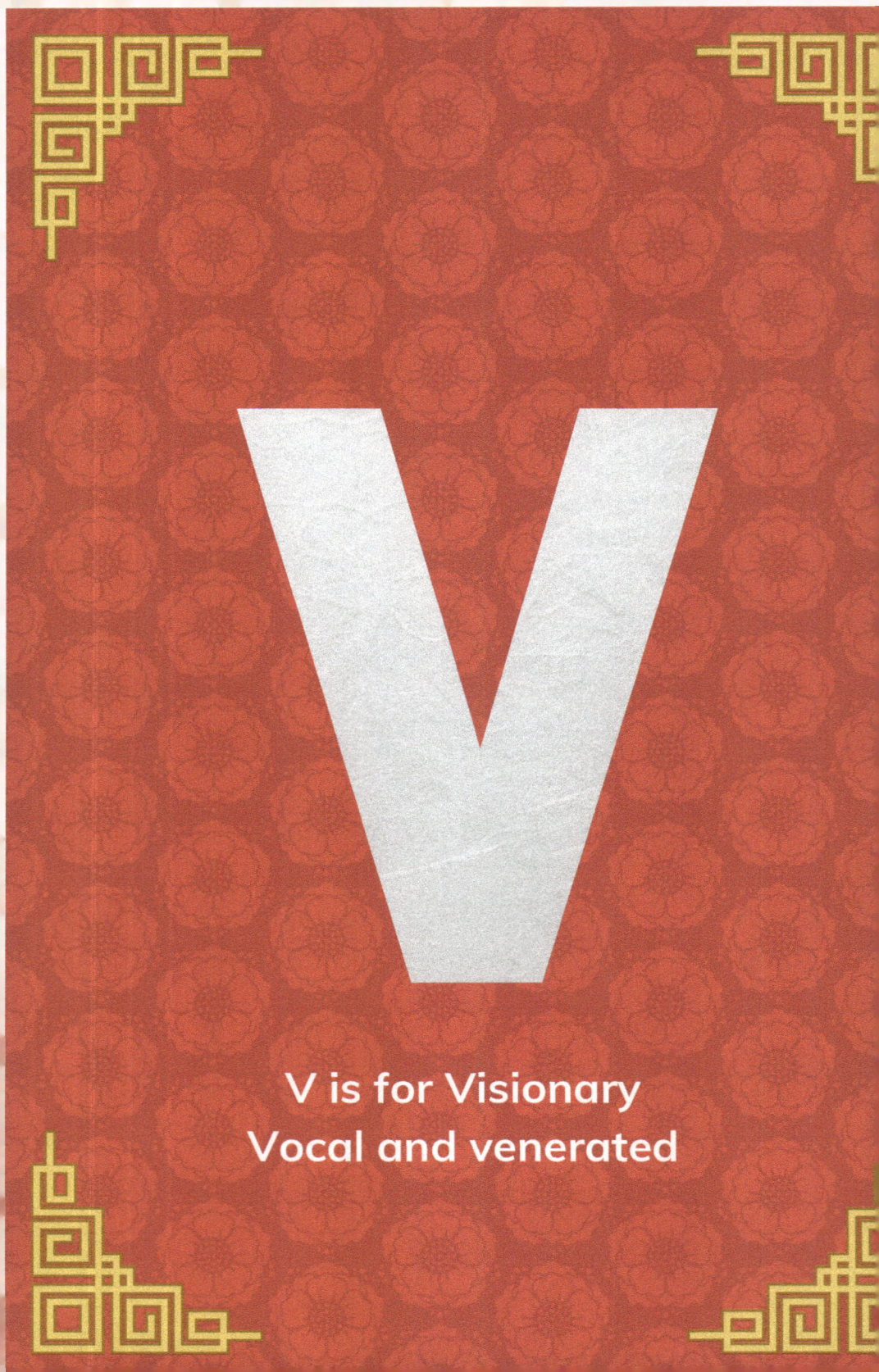

V

V is for Visionary
Vocal and venerated

Science and art grew under Seondeok's rule. She helped start schools and ordered the building of temples and pagodas. Some have survived until today.

Bunhwangsa Temple

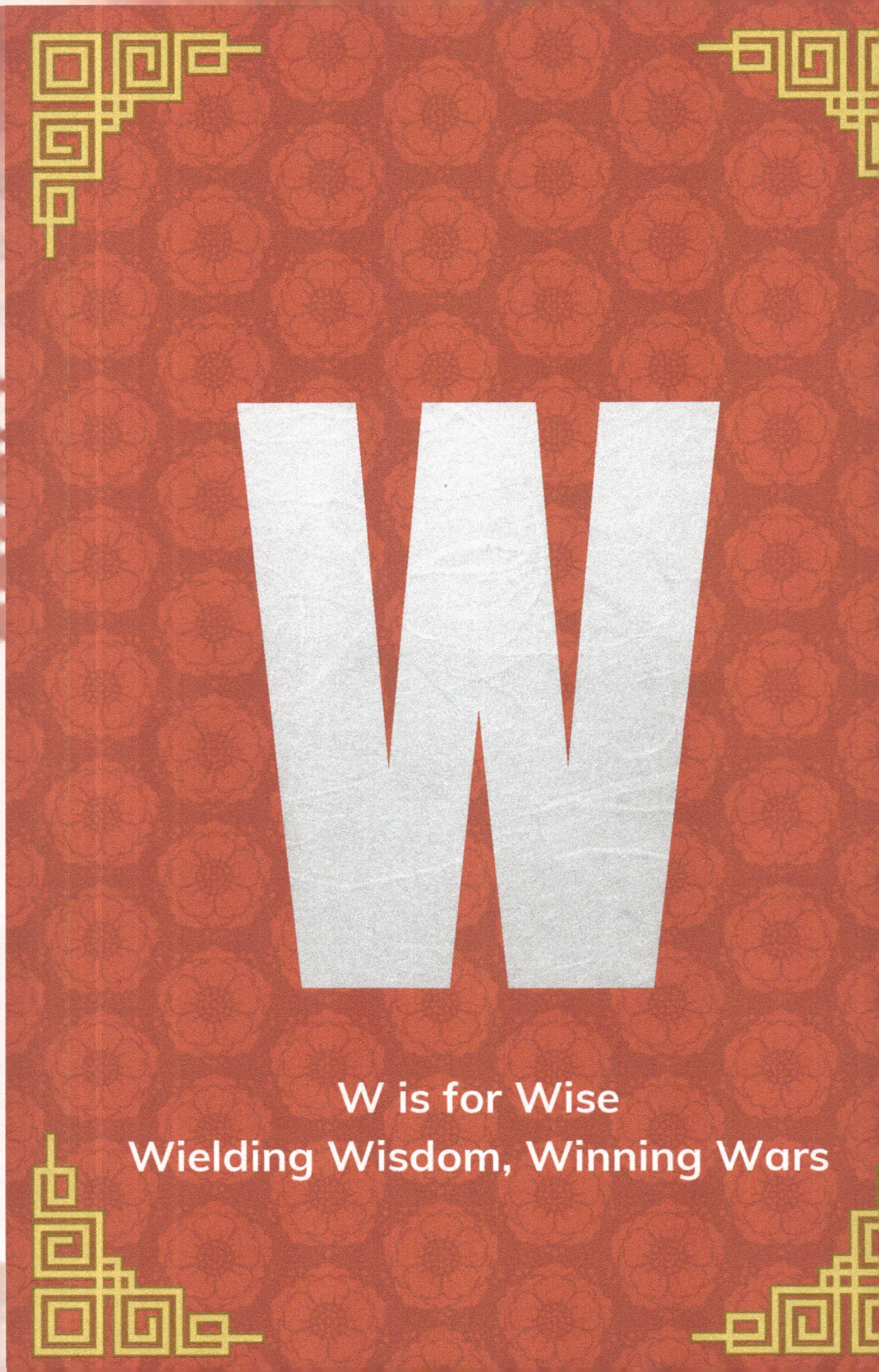

W

W is for Wise
Wielding Wisdom, Winning Wars

Korea has many legends about Seondeok. The stories show how wise she was. Sometimes, legends describe her ability to predict the future. They say she saw a comet that predicted an enemy attack..

X

X is for eXecuted enemies

Seondeok valued peace but knew she had to defend her kingdom. She sometimes had to go to war to defend Silla.

Y

Y is for Yeowang

Seondeok had many titles. Yeowang (Yuh-wahng) meant "Female King." From an early age, the Yeowang of Korea searched for knowledge. The female king loved to learn.

Z is for Zoetic

Queen Seondeok was a zoetic (lively) queen, filled with energy and passion. She worked hard to make Silla a better place. She had a deep zest for helping others.

More About Queen Seondeok

In Silla's Bone Rank system, you had to marry a person from your own bone-rank. You had to wear clothes made of certain fabrics and dyed certain colors. These rules even applied to small objects like hair pins and combs. Because of its rigid rules, Silla's Bone Rank system created a unique problem.

The Kingdom of Silla was founded in 57 BC/BCE. According to legend, there was once a small land called Saro. One day, the head of a village in Saro went to the well. He saw a white horse kneeling by the well and weeping. Curious, he drew closer and saw that the horse knelt next to an enormous purple egg. The shell cracked and out hatched a tiny child. The villagers named the boy Bak Hyeokgeose. On his thirteenth birthday, they crowned Hyeokgeose king of Saro. Eventually, the name of the kingdom changed from Saro to Silla. From Hyeokgeose to King Jinpyeong, every Silla ruler was a man.

But King Jinpyeong had no sons, only daughters. He, his wife, and his daughters were the only members of the sacred-bone rank. But only a member of the sacred-bone rank could rule Silla. What could he do? Seondeok, his daughter, asked for a chance to prove herself. Seondeok was wise and clever, and King Jinpyeong agreed.

Not everyone liked the king's decision. Several of his advisors plotted rebellion. The traitors were caught and executed, and Seondeok became the first queen of Korea in 632 AD/CE.

Many legends surround Seondeok. According to one story, a Chinese ambassador sent her a painting of peonies. These flowers were unknown in Korea at the time. When Princess Seondeok saw the painting, she admired their beauty. "It's sad that these beautiful flowers have no scent," she added. Royal gardeners planted the seeds that accompanied the painting. When the flowers bloomed, the court discovered the princess's prediction was correct. The flowers were lovely but had no scent. They asked Princess Seondeok how she had known. "If they had smelled sweet, there would have been bees and butterflies around the blossoms."

Queen Seondeok worked tirelessly for her people. She made the peasant class exempt from taxes for an entire year. She also ordered the construction of an astronomical observatory called Cheomseongdae. Its name means "Star-Gazing Tower." Besides observing the stars, scientists used it as a weather observatory. Farmers used weather observations from this tower to decide when to plant and harvest their crops.

Like her father, Queen Seondeok was a devout Buddhist. She funded the construction of temples and pagodas throughout the kingdom. One of the pagodas, Hwangnyongsa, was the tallest in the world at the time. Its name means Imperial Dragon Temple.

Queen Seondeok was unpopular with the other nobles. Many objected to having a female ruler. The Emperor of China even refused to recognize her as queen. Throughout her reign, there were several rebellions. In 647, one of her formerly loyal followers led the largest rebellion yet. The man, Bidam, said that she was not fit to rule and proved a woman should never be in charge. He thought that he could prove he was a better ruler by rebelling. Queen Seondeok succeeded in putting down the rebellion. She ordered the execution of Bidam and many of his followers.

She died later that year, likely because of illness. Some say she grew weak after Bidam's betrayal. Because she had not married, the throne passed to another queen: her cousin Jindeok. But neither Queen Jindeok nor her successor, Queen Jinseong, accomplished as much as the first queen of Korea

Learn more about medieval Korea with Korea Unboxed!
https://www.historyunboxed.com/seondeok

OTHER BOOKS BY HISTORY UNBOXED

Exploration Series
Ancient History: A Secular Exploration of the World (Volume 1) by Elizabeth Hauris and Stephanie Hanson
Medieval History: A Secular Exploration of the World (Volume 2) by Stephanie Hanson, Renee Corbino, and Rebecca McCormick (coming soon)
Ancient Eats: An Edible Exploration of the World by Stephanie Hanson
Boards & Bones: A Playful Exploration of the World by Stephanie Hanson (coming soon)

Historic Alphabet Biography Easy Readers
A is for Alexander by History Unboxed
C is for Charlemagne by History Unboxed
G is for Genghis Khan by History Unboxed

History Mystery Easy Readers
Mysteries of the Rubber People by Stephanie Hanson
Mysteries of the Shark Hunters by Elizabeth Hauris

Tales from Camelot
The Wizard and the Future King by Elizabeth Hauris and Stephanie Hanson

Coloring Books
Ancient History: A Coloring Comic Adventure by Stephanie Hanson and Elizabeth Hauris
Ancient History: A Coloring Penpal Adventure by Stephanie Hanson and Elizabeth Hauris

ABOUT HISTORY UNBOXED

Who We Are: An education company providing high-quality and engaging materials for learners of all ages.

Mission: To spark a love of history in children of all ages and lay the foundation for lifelong learning.

Vision: To provide opportunities for children to engage in the study of history through hands-on learning opportunities and fascinating books.

Core Values:

- Providing children with engaging learning materials that will spark their interest and serve to deepen their love of learning.
- Making history relatable, relevant, and exciting.
- Taking a global approach to history by discussing people and places often left out of traditional history materials.
- Going beyond dates and battles on a journey into a story that belongs to all of us — the history of peoples all over the world.
- Keeping materials secular and flexible to complement a variety of educational frameworks.
- Inspiring critical thinking about peoples and events of the past and facilitating deeper discussion in the student's educational environment.

www.ingramcontent.com/pod-product-compliance
Lightning Source LLC
Chambersburg PA
CBHW051334120626
46547CB00016B/2539